American Celebrations

John Willis

EYEDISCOVER

Go to www.openlightbox.com and enter this book's unique code.

BOOK CODE

AVA34695

EYEDISCOVER brings you optic readalongs that support active learning.

Published by Lightbox Learning Inc.
276 5th Avenue, Suite 704 #917
New York, NY 10001
Website: www.openlightbox.com

Library of Congress Control Number: 2022935957

ISBN 978-1-7911-4881-2 (hardcover)

Printed in Guangzhou, China
1 2 3 4 5 6 7 8 9 0 26 25 24 23 22

092022
102121

Project Coordinator: John Willis
Art Director: Terry Paulhus

The publisher acknowledges Getty Images and Shutterstock as the primary image suppliers for this title.

EYEDISCOVER provides enriched content, optimized for tablet use, that supplements and complements this book. EYEDISCOVER books strive to create inspired learning and engage young minds in a total learning experience.

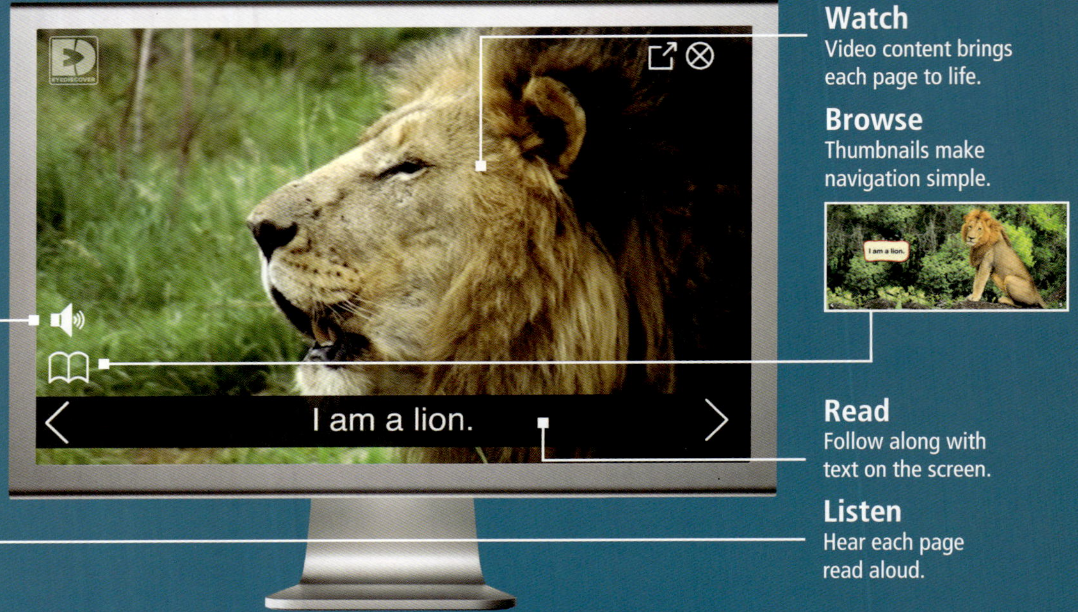

Watch
Video content brings each page to life.

Browse
Thumbnails make navigation simple.

Read
Follow along with text on the screen.

Listen
Hear each page read aloud.

Your EYEDISCOVER Optic Readalongs come alive with...

Audio
Listen to the entire book read aloud.

Video
High resolution videos turn each spread into an optic readalong.

OPTIMIZED FOR
- TABLETS
- WHITEBOARDS
- COMPUTERS
- AND MUCH MORE!

American Celebrations

In this book, you will learn about

• when they happen

• how people celebrate them

and much more!

People in the United States celebrate many days. Each celebration has its own meaning.

OLD NAVY
planet fitness

People come together for New Year's Eve on the last night of each year. They celebrate the start of a new year.

Presidents' Day is held each February. Schools and cities have events to teach people about past U.S. presidents.

PRESIDENTIAL LIBRARY AND MUSEUM
States of America

Americans gather on June 19 for Juneteenth. They celebrate the end of slavery in the United States.

Independence Day is on July 4. People celebrate the birth of the United States with parties and fireworks.

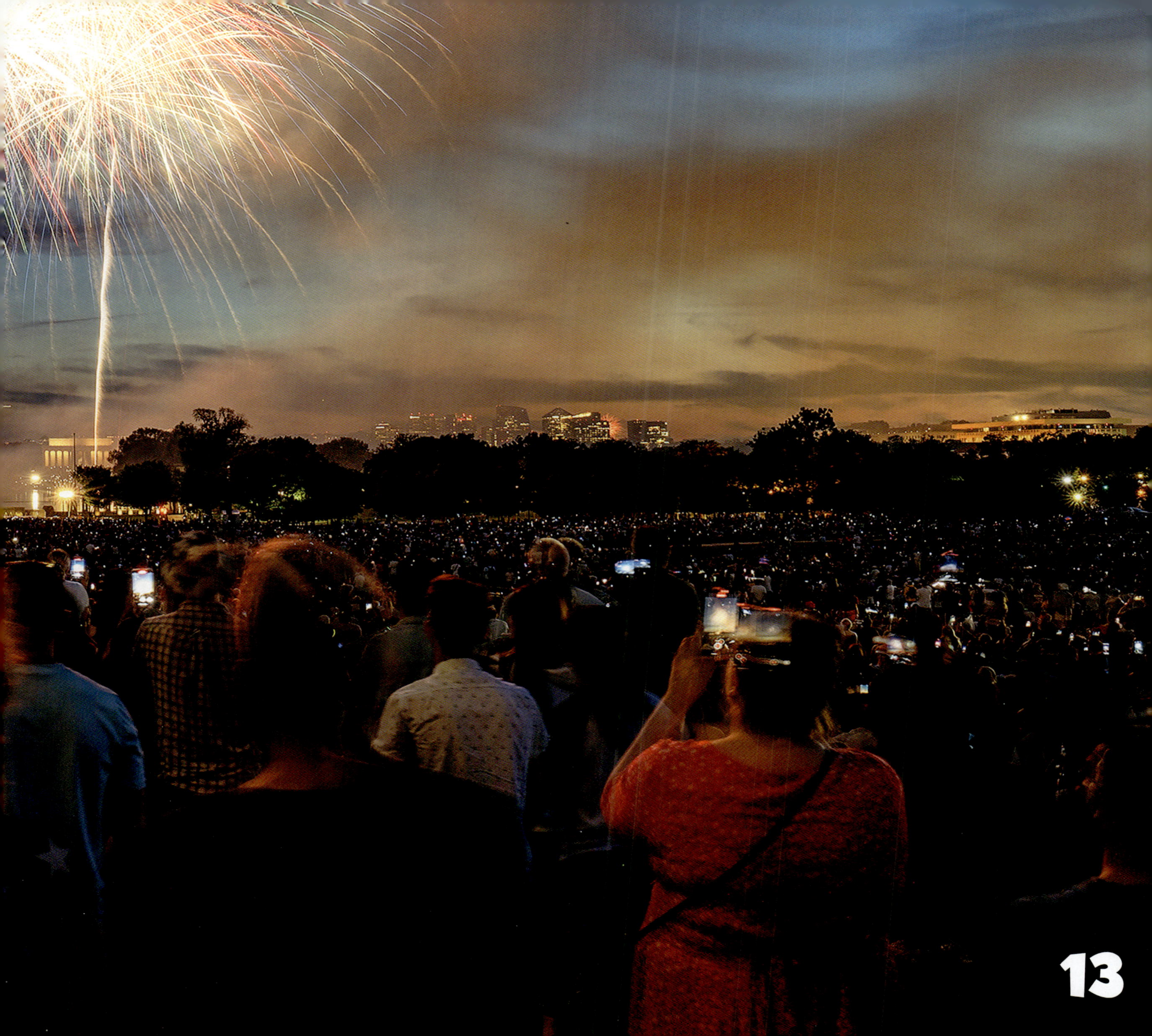

Halloween is on October 31. Children celebrate by wearing costumes and trick-or-treating.

Veterans Day is celebrated on November 11. It is a day to honor all Americans who have served in the military.

Thanksgiving takes place on the fourth Thursday of each November. Many families celebrate with a turkey dinner.

Americans celebrate many holidays in December. These include Christmas, Hanukkah, and Kwanzaa.

AMERICAN CELEBRATIONS BY THE NUMBERS

Christmas became a **FEDERAL HOLIDAY** in the United States in 1870.

Americans **spend** about **$600 million** on **turkeys** for each Thanksgiving.

About **45 PERCENT** of Americans **CARVE PUMPKINS** on Halloween.

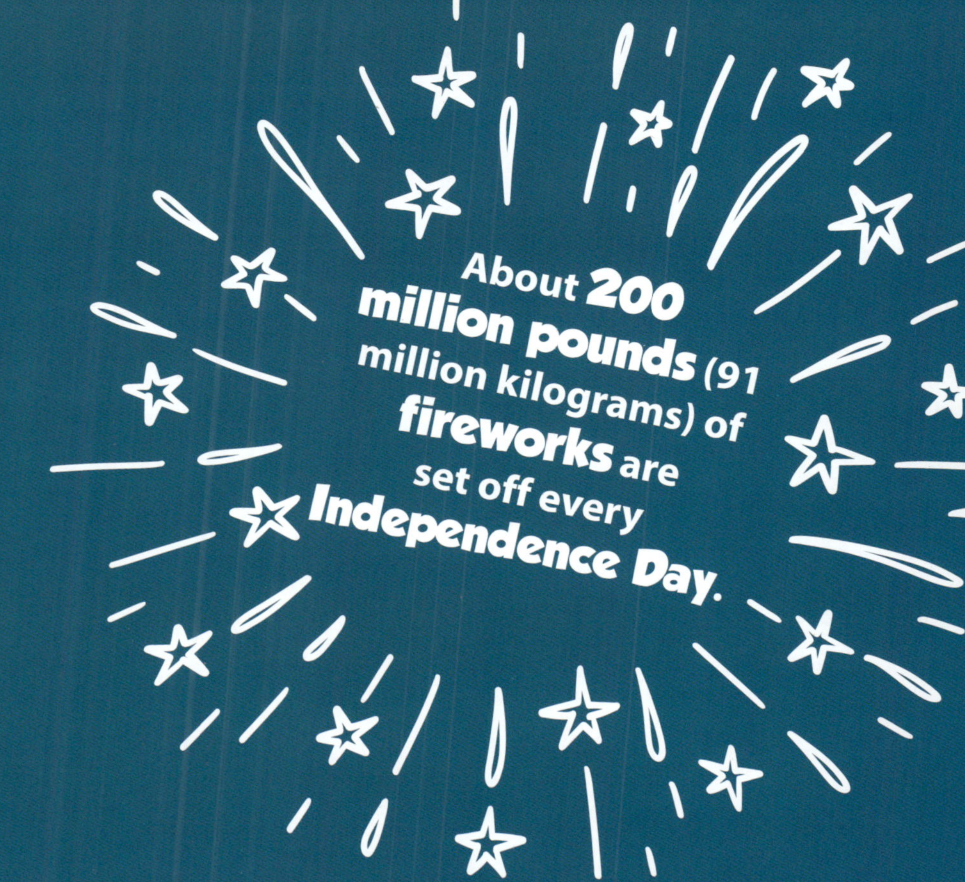

About **200 million pounds** (91 million kilograms) of **fireworks** are set off every **Independence Day.**

The **FIRST** known **New Year's celebrations** took place about **4,000 YEARS AGO.**

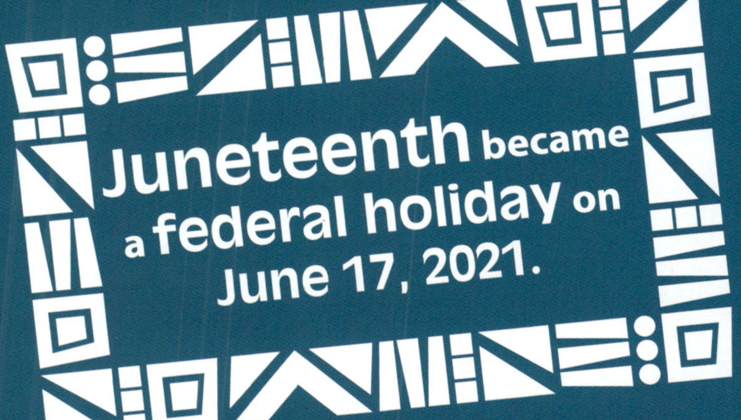

Juneteenth became a federal holiday on June 17, 2021.

KEY WORDS

Research has shown that as much as 65 percent of all written material published in English is made up of 300 words. These 300 words cannot be taught using pictures or learned by sounding them out. They must be recognized by sight. This book contains 40 common sight words to help young readers improve their reading fluency and comprehension. This book also teaches young readers several important content words, such as proper nouns. These words are paired with pictures to aid in learning and improve understanding.

Page	Sight Words First Appearance
4	days, each, has, in, its, many, own, people, states, the
7	a, come, for, last, new, night, of, on, start, they, together, year
8	about, and, have, is, schools, to
11	Americans, end
12	with
15	by, children, or
17	all, it, who
19	place, takes
20	these

Page	Content Words First Appearance
4	celebration, meaning, United States
7	New Year's Eve
8	events, February, presidents, Presidents' Day
11	June, Juneteenth, slavery
12	fireworks, Independence Day, July, parties
15	costumes, Halloween, October
17	military, November, Veterans Day
18	Thanksgiving, Thursday, turkey dinner
20	Christmas, December, Hanukkah, holidays, Kwanzaa

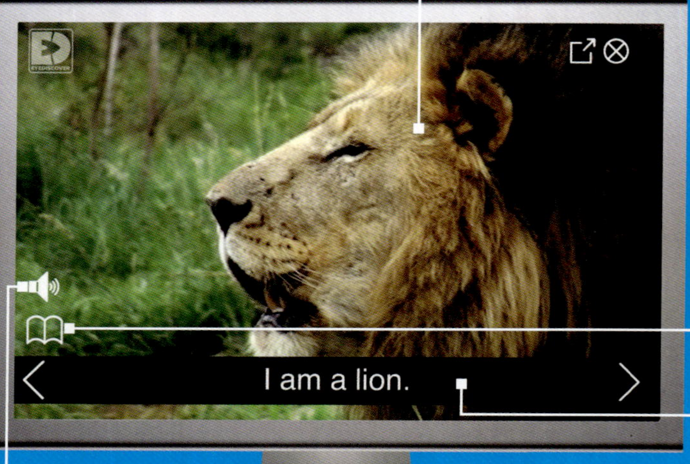

Watch
Video content brings each page to life.

Browse
Thumbnails make navigation simple.

Read
Follow along with text on the screen.

Listen
Hear each page read aloud.

Go to www.openlightbox.com and enter this book's unique code.

BOOK CODE

AVA34695